Dedication:
This book is dedicated to our Lord Jesus
Christ. It is through His death and resurrection
that each of us has the right to become an heir
in His kingdom. Thank you Lord for your
grace that has enabled me to put this book
together. May YOU be glorified.

ACKNOWLEDGMENTS

My deepest appreciation to. . .

Mrs. Hilda Caldwell, my high school English teacher. You taught me the skills needed to put this book together. Despite my complaints, all the *hard* work you assigned has paid off. Your love for the Lord always shined through in your smiling eyes. Thank you.

My parents, Roland and Lavada Owenby. Daddy, your zeal for studying Scripture has always encouraged me to dig deeper in the Word. Mama, your unwavering faith throughout my years has taught me that even in the deepest valleys and the most tempestuous storms our Lord is always there.

My faithful husband, Ron. Your encouragement while working on this book has been priceless. Having you as my resident computer expert was most helpful. Thank you for your love and patience. I love you.

My beautiful daughters, Missy and Jessica. Thank you for the sacrifices each of you has made in order for our family to follow the Lord's leading. You are both treasured gifts from God.

Angie, my biological as well as spiritual sister. Your faithful prayers have carried me through even when I didn't realize I needed to be carried.

Jess and Carol Jackson, my special friends. You happen to be my pastor and his wife but you are friends first. You have taught me so much not only through your preaching and teaching, but mostly by the examples you set in your daily walks with the Lord. Thank you for setting the right examples even when it is not the easy thing to do.

Jo Ann, David J., Lorenda, David B., Mary, Danny, Kathy, and many others who are my friends and faithful intercessors. You have stood with me through thick and thin. You have seen me at my best as well as my worst, yet you continue to love and encourage me. The hours of prayer spent with each of you are priceless. Your prayers and encouragement kept me pushing until this project was birthed.

Lorenda, Rob, and Carol E., my volunteer proofreaders. Lorenda, your attention to the details of mechanics such as style, grammar, and typos put the polishing touches on each page. Rob, your attention to the accuracy of Scripture and its use ensured a consistent theme with Biblical support. Carol, even though I was unable to obtain your corrections before moving overseas, your previous suggestions on other projects proved very valuable. All those corrections and remarks you each colorfully penned are deeply appreciated.

TABLE OF CONTENTS

FOREWORD

I am privileged to work with leaders all over the world who have a spiritual hunger to see transformation come to the cities where they live and spread the Good News. Therefore, many times I begin my day by asking the Lord to release His glory, establish His presence, and convert these cites from the kingdom of darkness to His glorious Kingdom of Light. In addition to my prayers, I often want to be able to meet with these spiritual leaders with the practical "how tos" they can use to begin the transformation process. For that reason, I am very excited about *Taking Possession of the Land.* This well-thought-out manual uses a logical one-two-three guide for prayer leaders or for any believer wanting to see true change come to where they live.

Acts 17:26,27 says, "And He has made from one blood every nation of men to dwell on all the face of the earth, and has determined their preappointed times and the boundaries of their dwellings, so that they should seek the Lord, in the hope that they might grope for Him and find Him, though He is not far from each one of us." What an important principle. God has placed us where we are so we can find Him. This important manual can help you do just that!

Any intercessor or prayer leader should use this manual so they are assured of accomplishing what the Lord has asked them to accomplish within their boundaries. This manual prevents you from scattering your prayers by giving you directives on prayerwalking, showing you how to record your prophetic declarations, and most importantly showing you how to remain accountable to secure the boundaries that the Lord has predetermined for you to be apart of. I am sure that this book will bless you, even as it has blessed me!

Chuck D. Pierce
Vice President, Global Harvest Ministries
Colorado Springs, Colorado

PREREQUISITE

Whether you are going through this manual on your own or as a member of a group, there is one prerequisite that must be met before beginning your work.

The land you are preparing to possess is yours to possess only if you are a child of God. This makes you an heir to this land. To become a child of God and therefore an heir, you must receive Jesus Christ as your Lord and Savior. Use the space below to share that experience.

If you do not have a testimony you can write here, or are not sure you have been born again into the family of God, would you like to receive Christ as Savior now and become a child of God? The process of becoming His child is simple but life changing:

- Agree with God that you are a sinner. (Romans 3:23)
- Tell God that you believe Jesus is the Son of God and that He died on the cross to give you eternal life. (John 1:1,14; Romans 5:8)
- Put all your trust in Jesus for eternal life. (Ephesians 2:8-9; Acts 4:12)
- Repent—ask Jesus to forgive you for your sins and determine to turn away from them. (1 John 1:9)
- Ask Jesus to be the Lord of your life.
- Thank God for providing the way through Jesus to eternal life and making you a joint heir with Jesus.

If you have just gone through these steps and have received Christ as your Savior, welcome to the Family! Please write out your commitment to the Lord below.

_____

_____

_____

_____

_____

_____

_____

Share this commitment with your pastor, Sunday school teacher, or other Christian that they may rejoice with you.

*If you are already a Christian, please pray for others who will read this who have not accepted Jesus as their Savior. Also pray for other people you know who need Jesus and those who will be touched by Jesus as a result of your working through this manual.

INTRODUCTION

He remembers his covenant forever, the word he commanded, for a thousand generations, the covenant he made with Abraham, the oath he swore to Isaac . . . . For he remembered his holy promise given to his servant Abraham. He brought out his people with rejoicing, his chosen ones with shouts of joy; he gave them the lands of the nations, and they fell heir to that others had toiled for. (Psalm 105:8-9, 42-44.)

God gave Canaan to the children of Israel as their inheritance. As descendants of Abraham this was their promised land, because the Lord had pledged it to them in a covenant made with Abraham (see Genesis 15:18).

We, too, are heirs to the land of the nations mentioned in Psalm 105. How? The first chapter of Matthew clearly states that Jesus is a descendant of Abraham. When we accept Jesus Christ as our Lord and Savior we become children of God, and thus joint heirs with Jesus. Thus, through Jesus we are heirs to the same inheritance given to Abraham's descendants (see Galatians 3).

Yet inheriting the land isn't easy. Often we delay the process through our disobedience and wandering from the Lord's path. The Israelites certainly discovered this. They had been slaves in Egypt for many years before God raised up Moses to set them free. Once out of bondage they were excited about moving into Canaan—their promised land. But the journey, which should have taken less than two weeks, instead took 40 years due to their failure to worship God alone and follow him wholeheartedly. It was not until God had a people committed to reaching the promised land at all costs—a whole generation later—that they crossed over the Jordan into Canaan.

What's more, God even redeems seemingly wasted time in preparing us to take the land. On the way to Canaan He used hardships such as famine and battles with various enemies to train His people and prepare them to take possession of their promised land. Even after moving into the promised land God's people continued to forsake Him. They allowed themselves to become captive to sin, preventing God in His holiness from communing with them. Yet God used even this betrayal to give His people victory. By sending His Son, Jesus, He provided the way for all of us to become children of God. Jesus' sacrifice enabled us to be joint heirs with Him and inherit a promised land even better than Canaan—the promised land of Heaven. Though Jesus came to set the captives free and lead them on their journey to this promised land, all the captives must be set free and all the nations subdued before crossing over.

Throughout Scripture God sets forth a pattern to follow in taking possession of land. In the Old Testament the land is physical land. In the New Testament, after Jesus provided for us to become his adopted heirs, the land became the field of souls throughout the world. This field is a spiritual one that can only be possessed by those who have accepted Jesus as Savior and Lord.

In this manual you will find a strategy for possessing the land step by step. Because the field of souls is so large, this is not a set of plans that will be carried out once, thus ending the process. We will need to continue repeating this strategy until Jesus comes. As this process is completed over and over, more of God's glory will be present and more people will determine to follow him.

Once all the people have been given the opportunity to follow Jesus, our Lord and Deliverer, out of bondage—which is sin and the world—He will return in glory to lead us across this new "Jordan" into heaven. Until then, the Holy Spirit will guide us like a cloud by day and a pillar of fire by night. The Lord has placed each of us in a "nation" that must be subdued. Just as he gave Abraham the inheritance of nations, He has given us the same inheritance through Jesus. So what are we waiting for? God is asking us the same question He asked the Israelites: "How long will you wait . . . ?" (Joshua 18:3). It is my desire to see all captives set free and all nations subdued so I can cross over the Jordan, led by the Holy Spirit, to meet my Deliverer and Father face to face. Let us wait no longer to take possession of the land the Lord has given us.

How to Use This Manual

Unlike other Bible studies, training materials, and books you may have used in the past, this manual may never be completed. The strategy outlined in this manual is a cycle that will be repeated throughout your life whether you are a new Christian or a seasoned one. It is a strategy on how to fulfill the Great Commission. Your study and use of the information given will continue until every person on earth has heard the Gospel of Jesus Christ, or until you are called home to be with the Lord in Heaven.

As you work through the manual, please complete all activities you are asked to do. Some things may seem somewhat unusual but are included to provide you with valuable practice in the things you will be called to do as you go out to possess the land the Lord has given you. So please, complete every activity no matter how odd, elementary, or difficult it may seem. You will not be asked to do anything that is not based on Scripture.

The manual is divided into phases, which are subdivided into steps. If you are using this with a small group, you may want to work through one phase per week. You should meet to go over what is expected of you before completing each phase. Follow-up should be done on the previous phase at each meeting. If you are leading a small group through this manual, be sure to complete the manual on your own before leading others through it.

If you are working through this on your own, take your time; some phases require more time than others. Spend at least a couple of days on each phase, but be prepared to take more time, if necessary. Each phase provides a stone on which the next is built, so you will want to be sure each phase is complete.

If you can, though, I encourage you to work with at least one other person because it provides you with a prayer partner. Set a time to meet weekly to review what you are doing, as well as to pray with and for one another. The more time you spend in prayer throughout the course of this training material, the more you will learn. This manual was written for people from various backgrounds, in differing circumstances, and in numerous places throughout the world. The time you spend in prayer will allow the Lord to personalize the material for you.

You will see the following symbols throughout the manual. They represent different activities you will be asked to do. Below is a legend for what each symbol represents. Be prepared to stop at each icon and spend time completing each activity.

 Prayer Activity

 Journal Entry

 Bible Reading

PHASE I
Locate the Land

STEP 1:
Start Where You Are

When the children of Israel were carried from their home in Jerusalem into exile in Babylon, the Lord told them:

Build houses and settle down, plant gardens and eat what they produce. . . . Increase in number there; do not decrease. Also, seek the peace and prosperity of the city to which I've carried you into exile. Pray to the Lord for it because if it prospers, you too will prosper. (Jeremiah 29:5-7)

The Lord wanted His people to be just as committed to working their land of exile as they were to working their homeland.

The Lord has placed you where you are. The Sovereign Creator of the Universe has seen fit for you to live in the city or county where your neighborhood is located. He has ordained your current street address. Whether temporarily or permanently, the Lord has planted you there. This is "the land" the Lord has called you to possess and occupy.

Many of us live where we are because this is where we have chosen to settle. This is where we plan to establish roots and homestead. Others of us are living where we are because of circumstances in our lives. Perhaps we are living in this particular area until we can afford to live somewhere else. Maybe we are living here because this is where our occupation leads us. My husband, Ron, is in the Navy, so we live wherever the Navy sends us. Some of us may actually feel like we are in exile and cannot wait to get back to our homeland. There have been times in my life when I have felt this way. Whatever our reasons for living where we are, the Lord calls us to do the same as the Israelites did in Babylon. We are to work the land and pray for the city.

Therefore, the first step in locating the land that your Father has given you to possess is to take note of where you live. Start with the plot of land where your home is located. The home and surrounding property should belong to the Lord. Ask Him if there is any work that needs to be done within your home in order for Him to completely possess it. He may lead you to remove things from your home that are unpleasing to Him. He may lead you to walk through your home and around your property to verbally claim it for His kingdom. Go to the Lord in prayer and ask Him what He would have you do. There is no set format to follow. Just be sensitive to the Holy Spirit.

If you live in a home with someone who does not know the Lord as Savior or who does not share your convictions of possessing the land, just be obedient to what the Lord tells you. The Lord is asking you to make a commitment; you are not responsible for the hearts of others. Listening to the Holy Spirit and being obedient is the key. The Lord knows your situation. Trust Him to guide you.

On the other hand, those of you who are blessed with Christian families may want to involve them in this process. Again, seek the Lord's face on what He would have you do and be obedient. Making a family commitment to possess the land will bring spiritual growth and unity to your family.

Prayer Activity

Spend some time alone with the Lord. Ask Him what things He would have you do to ensure that your property is His possession. You are setting up the home base from which you will carry out the phases set forth in this manual. Be prepared to just be quiet before the Lord and hear what He has to say to you.

*Take a few minutes to walk through your home and on your property. Ask the Lord to lead you to any items that need to be removed. Pray a prayer similar to the one below:

Father, thank You for the home You have given me. My home and everything in it I commit to You. If there is anything here that displeases You, reveal it to me. Because of my love for You and my desire to please You, I will remove it or change it. I want my home to be a home that You are comfortable in. Guide me Lord. Amen.

Journal Entry

Record the name or address of the plot of land the Lord has given you to possess:

_____

Record any thing you need to change or remove in order to take possession of the land.

_____

_____

STOP! Please do not go any further until you have completed the previous step. Taking possession of your property is crucial. Be sure your home belongs to the Lord. This will provide a safe haven for you to return to as you go out to possess the rest of the land the Lord has given you.

Step 2:
Size Up the Land

Now that you have established ownership and possession of your home and property, you are ready to begin taking possession of more land for the Lord. Spend some more time with the Lord and listen to His heart. Ask Him to reveal how far out He would have you go. What land is He giving you? Is He leading you to possess your:

- ✔ Street?
- ✔ Neighborhood?
- ✔ Community?
- ✔ Zip Code?
- ✔ City?
- ✔ County?
- ✔ State?
- ✔ Beyond?

Listen to the prompting of the Holy Spirit. The Lord will lead some to start with their street with no foreknowledge of whether the borders will ever extend beyond that. Others will start out being challenged to possess an entire city. Either way, your home will be the starting point for possessing any piece of land. Keep in mind that the apostles were told they would be witnesses first in Jerusalem, their home (see Acts 1:8). If the Lord leads you to possess a large piece of land like a city do not be overwhelmed. There will be others who will be called to work alongside you. God never calls us to a task without giving us what it takes to complete it. We just have to listen for His guidance and be obedient.

Whether we are called to take a street or an entire city for God, we are not alone. The Lord is calling others to do the same thing across our land. If each of us will do our part, led by the Holy Spirit and assisted by the entire body of Christ, every piece of land that we walk upon will belong once again to the Lord Jesus Christ. This will prepare the way for Jesus to come into our cities and towns in power—and might bring revival and spiritual awakening!

Prayer Activity

Ask the Lord how far out He would have you go in possessing the land. Keep in mind that this piece of land can be as large as a state or as small as a few houses on a street in your neighborhood. Pray something similar to the prayer below while making it personal for your particular circumstances.

Father, what land beyond my personal property would you have me take possession of? Thank You for giving me all I need to take possession of it. Amen.

Journal Entry

The Lord has called me to go beyond my personal property to possess more land for His kingdom. He has called me to possess the land of:

_____

PHASE II
Prepare to Go Forth
Into the Land

You are getting ready to move in and take possession of land the Lord has given you for an inheritance as His child. Anytime someone moves, whether moving across town or across the ocean, there are preparations to be made. You have already been working on getting your current residence squared away, but now you need to make sure that you as an individual are prepared. Just as you would not move into a new house without preparing yourself for the physical and mental stress it brings, you should not move out to take possession of the land the Lord has given you without preparation.

The children of Israel had to make preparations, too, before crossing the Jordan to possess the promised land. In Joshua 1:6-7, God told Joshua:

Be strong and courageous, because you will lead these people to inherit the land I swore to their forefathers to give them. Be strong and very courageous. Be careful to obey all the law my servant Moses gave you; do not turn from it to the right or to the left, that you may be successful wherever you go. (Joshua 1:6-7)

Joshua was to lead the children of Israel in to possess the land God had given them, but before crossing the Jordan he sent word through the camp to gather supplies and prepare themselves (see Joshua 1:10-11). Then, the day before crossing the Jordan they were to consecrate themselves (see Joshua 3:5). We should follow this example.

STEP 1:
Consecrate Yourself

Before taking possession of the land our Father has given us we must consecrate ourselves. To consecrate means to dedicate or perfect, which in turn means to make complete or without fault, to devote solemnly to a purpose.

We must dedicate ourselves to this purpose of possessing the land, for our dedication will be what helps us persevere when times get tough. We first need to spend time in prayer asking the Lord to cleanse us. We should ask him to remove everything that is unclean and repent of any unconfessed sin. In Psalm 51 David speaks of needing to be cleansed of his sin before he asks the Lord to rebuild the walls of Jerusalem. Cleansing and perfecting had to take place before the work.

Dedication also means setting apart. In Acts, for example, the apostles set apart seven men to be deacons (see Acts 6). We must also be set apart for the ministry and mission of possession. Making a commitment to dedicate yourself to possessing the land is serious. The Lord expects clean hearts and single-mindedness toward His ways. He wants people set apart for the work. When the Lord called Abram in Genesis 12, He told him to leave his country, his people, and his family. The Lord wanted him to be separate—set apart. In a similar way, we need to be spiritually set apart from anything that would entangle us. It is with God's help that we do this (see 1 Thessalonians 5:23-24). Spend as much time as necessary with the Lord working through any issues such as unforgiveness, fear, unconfessed sin, etc., as part of your preparation to take possession of the property.

Any work we do will be much more productive if we are consecrated and dedicated to the call.

Prayer Activity

Spend a significant amount of time with the Lord committing yourself to moving in and possessing the land. If you do not feel you have enough time to commit to this right now, set a date and time to do this activity within the next week.

1. Schedule time. (If not today, fill in when:

_____)

2. Sit quietly before the Lord meditating on the task at hand.

3. Pray, offering all of yourself to His service. (Do not take this lightly. Your commitment here is crucial to your ability to follow through with what the Lord leads you to do.)

4. After determining in your heart to be consecrated, or set apart, for this work sign the following commitment.

I, _____, consecrate myself, for the purpose of possessing the land my Lord has given me. I am willing to commit my time, resources, and strength to this calling. I will daily seek guidance from the Lord as my Commander. I am determined that with the help of the Holy Spirit and by the power of Jesus I will persevere in this calling until the land is completely possessed for Christ's kingdom.

Signed_____   Date_____

STEP 2:
Gather Supplies

Several times the Lord tells his people, "Be strong and courageous" (Deut. 31:23, Joshua 1:6, 1 Chron. 22:13). Usually, He tells them this before sending them in to take land from the enemy that the Lord has given them. Yet before going in, the soldiers must dress themselves in the proper clothing and armor in order to completely take the land. They also must learn to use their weapons.

Paul too encourages us, as Christians living after the resurrection of Christ with the presence of the Holy Spirit;

Finally, be strong in the Lord and in his mighty power. Put on the full armor of God so that you can take your stand against the devil's schemes (Ephesians 6:10-11).

Even though the Lord has given us the land, taking possession of it will be a spiritual battle. Satan, the prince of this world, wants to stay in control. He tries to interfere with the spreading of the Gospel, because he knows that if God's people take possession of the land he will lose control and God's kingdom will multiply. Therefore, he is going to fight anything we do to possess the land for Christ. We must remember, though, that;

. . . our struggle is not against flesh and blood, but against the rulers, against the authorities, against the powers of this dark world and against the spiritual forces of evil in the heavenly realms (Ephesians 6:12).

We must be ready for spiritual battle at any time. This is one of the reasons a clean heart is so important. We want nothing to get in the way of our effectiveness on the field.

Any time we are out doing the Lord's work we are on a battlefield. Though we must be strong and courageous as the Lord says, we must first arm ourselves with the weapons of His warfare that are issued to us at salvation. We have to learn how to put them on and use them. An equipment list, along with instructions, is included in Ephesians 6:10-18. We must daily follow these guidelines of putting on the full armor of God and taking up our weapons. The courage and strength the Lord tells us to have will come more easily when this is done.

You may memorize the following checklist, use your Bible as a checklist, or create your own using the Scriptures. Whatever format your checklist takes, be sure to verbally go through it before venturing out each day.

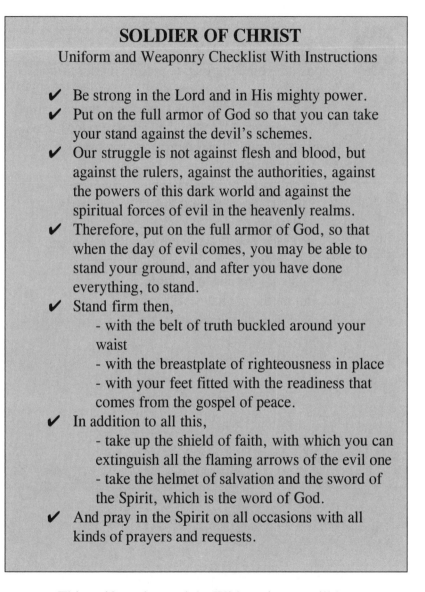

SOLDIER OF CHRIST

Uniform and Weaponry Checklist With Instructions

✔ Be strong in the Lord and in His mighty power.

✔ Put on the full armor of God so that you can take your stand against the devil's schemes.

✔ Our struggle is not against flesh and blood, but against the rulers, against the authorities, against the powers of this dark world and against the spiritual forces of evil in the heavenly realms.

✔ Therefore, put on the full armor of God, so that when the day of evil comes, you may be able to stand your ground, and after you have done everything, to stand.

✔ Stand firm then,
- with the belt of truth buckled around your waist
- with the breastplate of righteousness in place
- with your feet fitted with the readiness that comes from the gospel of peace.

✔ In addition to all this,
- take up the shield of faith, with which you can extinguish all the flaming arrows of the evil one
- take the helmet of salvation and the sword of the Spirit, which is the word of God.

✔ And pray in the Spirit on all occasions with all kinds of prayers and requests.

This uniform is crucial. Without it you will be exposed to all the elements. You will have no defense against the enemy. He knows when our uniform is incomplete or missing, so put on the full armor of God and let's get ready to go into the field.

Prayer Activity

Let us take time to practice putting on our armor. Standing is not required to do this, but let us stand for this exercise to help us experience this as a true act. As you read through the following steps, read them aloud and act out putting on each piece.

1. I stand firm
2. With the belt of truth buckled around my waist,
3. With the breastplate (vest) of righteousness across my chest,
4. With my feet fitted with the gospel of peace (my boots).
5. I pick up the shield of faith,
6. Put on the helmet of salvation,
7. And pick up the sword of the Spirit (the Word).

Step 3:
Keep a Log

As you are going through the process of working your land, you will want to keep a log of what the Lord reveals to you. You will learn things from prayer, Bible study, research of your land, and in many other ways. As you spend time with the Lord He will reveal more of Himself to you. A journal will give you the opportunity to record all the things God shows you. You will be able to look back through your journal periodically and see how the Lord has worked in your life.

Your journal can be kept in any fashion you would like. You could buy one from a bookstore, such as a composition notebook or binder, or create one yourself. You could also keep your journal using word processing software on a computer.

 ## Journal Entry

Begin your journal by recording any insight the Lord may already be giving you in the space below. You can transcribe this into your journal later if you choose, along with all the other entries you have made in this manual.

_____

_____

_____

_____

STEP 4:
Attend Daily Briefings

To be an effective soldier, you must take time out to spend with the Commander (the Lord) each day. As you spend time with Him at the beginning of the day, God will reveal His plans for you and give you orders to be carried out. This would also be a good time to put on your uniform. He will inspect it to insure it is fitting properly, complete without holes, and not missing any pieces, but it will be your responsibility to go to Him daily for the inspection. You will also be responsible for keeping your uniform and weapons in good condition. Prayer, as mentioned in the instructions, will serve as the oil used to condition your equipment: "Pray in the Spirit on all occasions with all kinds of prayers and requests" (Ephesians 6:18).

During these briefings you will also want to consult your Bible. In it you will learn plans and strategies soldiers before you have used, which ones were successful, and why. Allow the Lord to teach you during these daily briefings.

STEP 5:
Pray for the People

Paul encourages us in 1 Timothy 2:1: ". . . first of all, that requests, prayers, intercession, and thanksgiving be made for everyone." Begin praying for the Lord to give you a compassion for the inhabitants of your land—both Christian and non-Christian. Ask Him to help you see the people as He sees them. Many of the people inhabiting the land are lonely, lost, and in bondage, and Jesus wants to set them free.

Throughout Scripture the prayers of God's people are the forerunners of His deliverance. Even the deliverance of the children of Israel from Pharoah's rule began with a prayer. The Bible tells us that:

The Israelites groaned in their slavery and cried out, and their cry for help because of their slavery went up to God. God heard their groaning and he remembered his covenant with Abraham, with Isaac and with Jacob. So God looked on the Israelites and was concerned about them (Exodus 2:23-25).

Many times the Lord spared Israel because of the prayers of men like Moses, Joshua, Isaiah, and Ezekiel.

When Jerusalem sinned against God, He said, "I looked for a man among them who would build up the wall and stand before me in the gap on behalf of the land..." (Ezekiel 22:30). The Lord is looking for those who are willing to stand in the gap for the people of the land. The fact that you have gotten this far into this strategy shows your desire to be one who stands in that gap. You are one of those for whom God has been searching.

The early church in Acts began the process of reaching the cities with prayer (see Acts 1:13-15a and 2:42). Of course, they did not have books written on the subject or seminars to attend to learn how; they simply joined with those of like mind to pray.

 Prayer Activity

Nehemiah prays for the people of Jerusalem in Nehemiah 1:4-10. Read this passage to get an idea of the type of prayer to pray for the people. Use this prayer as a guide and write out your own prayer for the people of your land.

_____

_____

_____

_____

_____

_____

_____

_____

Prayer starts the process of God's people occupying the land. Enlist a prayer partner to join you in your prayers for the people. This prayer partner can be someone from your church, someone in your neighborhood, or any Christian who also wants to see the community reached for Christ. A prayer partner will help you stay consistent in your prayer life as well as encourage you when things look less than encouraging.

You will learn more about the importance of prayer partners later on. It is good to go ahead and enlist your prayer partner(s) now. Choose at least one prayer partner but feel free to enlist as many as the Lord leads you.

 Journal Entry

My prayer partner(s) are:

_____

_____

_____

_____

Phase I & II
Progress Report

Date: —————————————————

Directions: Check all activities that have been completed.

_____ 1. I have located my land.
_____ 2. I have made sure my home and property are cleansed and set apart for the Lord.
_____ 3. I have established the size of the property the Lord has given me.
_____ 4. I have consecrated myself to be used by the Lord.
_____ 5. I have put on my uniform and taken up my weapons.
_____ 6. I have started praying for the people of the land.
_____ 7. I have enlisted a prayer partner.
_____ 8. I have started a personal journal.

If you have done each of these things you are ready to move on to the next step of the strategy. Go out into the land and survey it. Explore and see what's there.

PHASE III
Study the Land

Before taking ownership of a new home, the land must be surveyed to establish the location of the borders. This survey sometimes includes any fixtures on the property as well as any natural bodies such as lakes, streams, etc. It may also include any rights that the city, utility companies or others may have to certain areas for maintenance purposes. A similar survey needs to be carried out when we are preparing to take possession of the land God has given us.

God's people have been surveying their "promised land" throughout history. There are examples all through scripture of the Lord sending people out into the land before possessing it. The first mention of this is Genesis 13. God promises land to Abraham and his offspring forever. God then commands Abraham, in verse 17, to "Go, walk through the length and breadth of the land for I am giving it to you". This is quite possibly the very first prayerwalk ever recorded.

The Lord also instructs Moses to send men to explore the land of Canaan in Numbers 13:1-2. All through the Israelites' journey to the Promised Land, the Lord instructs his leaders to send spies into the lands they were getting ready to overtake and possess (see Deut. 1:21-23, Numbers 13:3, Joshua 2:1, and Joshua 18:8). These spies went into the land to see the layout of the terrain. They went to see what provisions were available. They also went in to observe the armies they would be going up against. It is always a good idea to know the strengths and weaknesses of your enemy. The information obtained by the spies was used in making decisions for the next step in taking possession of the Promised Land.

Paul quite often sent Timothy or one of his other companions ahead of him to cities. Could it be that they went ahead of Paul to survey and spy out the land? We can be sure that these men prayed and observed what was going on in these cities.

Surveying the land is necessary to know what needs to be done in order to possess the land the Lord has given you. In order to possess the land you need to become a surveyor. You need to become a spy. You need to let the Lord show you the land He has given you. You must then follow his directions on how to possess it.

At this point you should have completed the process of locating and preparing to move out into your land. You are now ready to go out and survey the land. There are many ways to do this. A combination of several ways usually produces the best results.

STEP 1:
Obtain a Map

One way to study the land is through the use of maps. Ezekiel is told by the Lord in Ezekiel 4:1 to "...take a clay tablet, put it in front of you and draw the city of Jerusalem on it." Ezekiel was told to draw a map of the city where the children of Israel were living. Ezekiel was then to lay siege to or take possession of the city. The map represents the city that Ezekiel was called to serve.

You can use maps similar to this as you survey your land. Most of you will be able to purchase maps that can be used. Studying these maps will help you learn the layout of the land. The size and location of your land will determine what types of maps will be available to you. If no pre-made maps are available, hand drawn maps of smaller areas will be sufficient. Experiment with making photocopies and enlarging or reducing copies of maps if you have a hard time finding a map of just your land.

Below is a sample list of sources for maps:
>Bookstores
>Libraries
>Tourist centers
>Chamber of Commerce
>Software Programs
>Phone books
>The Internet
>City zoning offices
>Fire departments
>Police departments

Once you have obtained a map you can utilize it in several ways. You can use it to mark off areas as you pray for those parts of your land to insure that an area is completely covered in prayer. You can also mark strongholds on the map. Strongholds will be explained further in Phase III. Later on you may use the map as a tool when working with others in the body. Your map will prove to be a great reference tool.

There are many ways to mark your map. The size of your map and the purposes for which it is used will determine how you want to mark it. You can keep it as simple as marking it with colored pens or pencils. You may choose to laminate your map. This will make it more durable. You can also use colored stickers on a laminated map without damaging it. Do not be surprised if you have your map for a while before the Lord leads you to do anything other than refer to it. Keep in mind that God's timing is perfect. Do not rush ahead of Him.

 ## Prayer Activity

Draw a sample map of your land (see next page). It doesn't have to be exact. A rough sketch will be good enough. It can have as many or as few details as you want.

To represent your laying siege to or possessing your land, lay your hand on the map you've drawn. Pray this prayer or a similar one:

Father, by the authority given to me as your child and by the power given to me through the blood of Jesus, I lay siege to the land of _____. Anyone occupying this land who is not willing to recognize you as Lord will have to accept you as such or be removed. I am laying siege ramps to overtake this land for the Lord, Jesus Christ.

Sample Map:

Step 2:
Prayerwalk the Land

Another way to survey the land is through prayerwalking. Prayerwalking is "praying on-site with insight." It is simply praying in the very places we expect God to bring forth his answers. It is putting feet to our prayers. We take the same prayers that we may be praying in our prayer closets and pray them close to the people and places we are asking the Lord to touch.

Earlier we discussed Abraham's walking the land the Lord had given him. Jesus prayed as he was out walking in the city. There is an account of what I believe to be a prayerwalking experience in Acts 8.

 Bible Reading
Read Acts 8:26-40

1. Who spoke to Philip?

2. What was Philip to do?

3. As Philip walked along he was spoken to again. By whom?

4. What was Philip told to do this time?

5. What happened after Philip was obedient to do
    what he was told? vv. 35-38

The Lord told Philip to travel the desert road from
Jerusalem to Gaza. As he did, the Holy Spirit told him to
stand near a man sitting beside the road. Because Philip
obeyed the Lord's instruction, the eunuch was saved.
Keep in mind that Philip's listening to the Holy Spirit was
prayer. Prayerwalking is really being obedient in what the
Lord tells you to do as you travel along.

Walk the land God has given you asking him to let
you see it through his eyes. It will not only bring you
closer to the people living in your neighborhood, community, and city, but it will also play a part in your staking a
claim for Jesus on the property. God says in Deut. 11:24
and in Joshua 1:3 that ". . . every place where you set
your foot will be yours."

There are two goals when prayerwalking: 1) to pray
blessings upon the land and people who surround you; and
2) to discern and remove the enemy and his influence. As
you walk through the land praying, you will not only be
petitioning the Lord on behalf of the people, but you will
be praising Him for what He is doing throughout the land.
As you praise the Lord and pray blessings for others, the
Light of Jesus shines where you are. Wherever there is
light, the darkness cannot remain. There may be times the
Lord will prompt you to specifically pray against the

demonic forces in your land. The shining of the Light will reveal these forces and quite often dispel them.

You may find a prayer guide helpful as you prayerwalk. Several are listed in the resource section of this manual. If you have never prayerwalked, you may want to read *Prayerwalking: Praying On-Site with Insight* by Steve Hawthorne and Graham Kendrick.[1]

It is always a good idea to take a partner with you when you prayerwalk. Having someone with you allows you to pray out loud while it appears to those around you that you are in conversation with your companion. A partner will also help you stay focused on the task at hand; he or she may sense some prayer needs that you do not sense.

As you prayerwalk, the Lord will show you things He is not pleased with on the property He has given you. Satan may have strongholds set up throughout the land, and you will want to mark them on your map and record them in your journal as you discover them. Some strongholds will be very obvious as you walk along, but others may be more subtle. For example, sometimes you may just feel uncomfortable about an area you are in. This discomfort may be the Holy Spirit within you discerning the presence of darkness. When this happens ask the Lord to show you the truth about the place and why you are not at peace there. He is always faithful to answer our questions.

When you are in a place like this, ask the Lord what you are to do. He may just be revealing something to you so you can record it and deal with it at a later date. Or, He may want you to pray in Jesus' name and by His blood that the powers of darkness leave that place and that the light and truth of Jesus prevail there.

Each situation will be different, so listen to the Holy Spirit for guidance. At times like these you will want to be sure that you have put your spiritual armor on so you will be fully equipped for what the Lord tells you to do. Remember never to do anything of your own prompting. Wait for the leading of the Lord and always do whatever you are led to do in the name of Jesus and by the power of His blood.

Some samples of strongholds are listed below:

Strongholds of Satan
- ✔ Pornographic businesses
- ✔ Bars and night clubs
- ✔ Gambling facilities
- ✔ Haunted houses or houses of horror
- ✔ Psychic or spiritualist establishments
- ✔ Masonic lodges
- ✔ Known witches' covens
- ✔ New Age facilities
- ✔ "Churches" that do not teach the truth of Jesus

Strongholds of the Lord
- ✔ Churches preaching and proclaiming the true gospel of Jesus
- ✔ Christian ministries
- ✔ Homes of Christian families
- ✔ Christian businesses
- ✔ Neighborhood houses of prayer
- ✔ Evangelistic billboards and signs

Of course, this list is just a starting point. You may find plenty of other things that would fit into either of these categories.

Keep in mind: It is not our mission to single-handedly subdue the land. Rather, it is our job to do whatever the Lord tells us to the best of our ability. If each member of the body of Christ will do his or her part, the land will be easily possessed for the Lord.

Prayer Activity

Set up a date for a prayerwalk. Contact your prayer partner and ask if he/she would like to join you. Go on this prayerwalk soon. The purpose is to get a general feel for what is on your land and what the Lord says about it. Just walk, pray, and listen.

Date of
prayerwalk:_____

What part of the land will be prayerwalked?

Things to take on your prayerwalk:
- ✔ Small notebook or pad of paper
- ✔ Pen or pencil
- ✔ Pocket Bible
- ✔ Comfortable shoes

Journal Entry

Record any information you retrieved about the land while you were out prayerwalking.

_____

_____

_____

_____

_____

_____

List any strongholds discovered—and whether they are of the Lord or Satan.

_____

_____

_____

_____

_____

Mark these strongholds on your map. Use a different color sticker or pencil for each type of stronghold. You may also use a symbol to represent whether the strongholds belong to God or Satan.

Notes
1. Steve Hawthorne and Graham Kendrick, *Prayerwalking: Praying On-Site with Insight* (Orlando FL: Creation House, 1993), p.12.

Step 3:
Research the Land

Along with mapping and prayerwalking you will also want to research your land. You need to learn the history of it and God's purpose for it. Why did the first people to settle here choose this place? Was it a Godly purpose?

You will also want to know things like the demographics of your land. For example, how many different cultural and racial groups live there? What have interracial relationships been like in the past? Has there been bloodshed on this land during time of war or at any other time?

If the land was settled for Godly reasons, you need to learn if those purposes have been carried out over the years. The Lord will use the information you gather to help you pray more effectively for the inhabitants of the land.

The best place to go to gather information on the history of the land is the local public library. School libraries will also be helpful if you have access to one. You could also talk to the older citizens of your land, or look for opportunities to join in local history classes and seminars. You will be amazed what you learn if you just keep your eyes and ears open.

You are not doing this research just to have more information. As you do the research try to do it through spiritual eyes. Be sure to wear your armor. Do not give the enemy an opportunity to distract you. Ask the Lord to show you information that is helpful to you, such as anything that has had an impact on how things are done in your land.

And remember, be sure to record spiritual insights in your journal or a separate notebook.

 ## Journal Activity

Go to the local library. Try to discover how the land was established. Record who the founders were and the purpose for settling on this land. Use the space below or your personal journal to record information you learn.

_____

_____

_____

_____

_____

_____

_____

_____

_____

_____

PHASE III
Progress Report

Date: _____

Directions: Check off all activities that have been completed or are in progress.

____ 1.   I have obtained a map of the land.
____ 2.   I have prayerwalked the land at least once to discover what is there.
____ 3.   I have recorded findings from prayerwalk(s) in my journal.
____ 4.   I have prayed with my prayer partner.
____ 5.   I have marked the strongholds found throughout the land on my map.
____ 6.   I have been consistently meeting with the "Commander" to receive his orders.
____ 7.   I have been consistently wearing my uniform and using my weapons.

Even if you have not completed every item on this list, you can still move on into the next phase. However, you will want to make sure that you continue to work on these steps as you go along. Numbers 6 and 7 are very important. As you complete an item, be sure to check it off the list.

PHASE IV
Join Other Heirs
of the Land

STEP 1:
Go in Together

If you are not doing so already, it is time to begin working with others in the body of Christ to take possession of the land the Lord has given you. All the children of Israel were heirs to the promised land as Abraham's offspring. You, as the offspring of Christ, through the blood He shed on the cross, are heirs to this land.

You are all sons of God through faith in Christ Jesus, for all of you who were baptized into Christ have clothed yourselves with Christ. There is neither Jew nor Greek, slave nor free, male nor female, for you are all one in Christ Jesus. If you belong to Christ, then you are Abraham's seed, and heirs according to the promise. (Galatians 3:26-29)

As an heir you have authority to possess the land. Every child of God has the right to take possession of the land, so we must all work at possessing it. God's word encourages us to work in unity with the rest of the Body of Christ. Each of us has a part to play. Ephesians 4:16 says, "From him the whole body, joined and held together by every supporting ligament, grows and builds itself up in love, as each part does its work." As each part of the Body does its part, we will be strengthened individually and corporately.

We have been referring to the children of Israel throughout this manual. Notice they are called the children of Israel not the child of Israel. God chose to have them go into Canaan, their promised land, together to take possession of it. In Numbers 32 we read the account of the Reubenites and Gadites requesting permission to settle on the east side of the Jordan in Jazer and Gilead regions before ever crossing over into Canaan. This chapter illustrates the commitment level and spirit of unity that is required to possess the land. Please take time to complete the following Bible Activity.

 Bible Reading

Read Numbers 32 and answer the following questions.

1. Why did these two tribes want to settle east of the Jordan?

2. Moses reminded them of a time in history when another set of men did not want to enter the promised land. Who were these men and why did they not want to enter the land?

3. What happened as a result of their fear and unwilling hearts?

4. What did the Reubenites and Gadites agree to do in order to keep the same thing from happening again?

These two tribes wanted to settle east of the Jordan because they saw that the land there was good for raising livestock. When Moses reminded them of the 40 years of wandering their ancestors endured after refusing to go into the promised land, the two tribes agreed to continue to fight along with the other ten for the possession of the promised land. Moses still permitted the tribes to settle east of the Jordan, but first they had to help their fellow Israelites take the land.

God desires all of His children to be involved in taking possession of the land. As we work in unity toward possessing the land God has given us, our goal will be accomplished.

There are many opportunities to work with other heirs of the land. A few of them will be discussed in this phase. The more you are involved with others in possessing the land the more productive your work will be.

STEP 2:
Enlist a Prayer Partner

You have already been advised and instructed to recruit a prayer partner. You should have already recorded the person's name in Phase II. If you have not done this yet, you need to do so now.

Having a prayer partner works quite a bit like the buddy system. Most of us are familiar with the buddy system as something used by kindergarten teachers on field trips to make sure that none of the children get lost and that each child will have a companion on the journey. Moreover, if the buddies are matched up effectively they will keep one another out of trouble. A prayer partner relationship works much in the same way.

There are many examples of partnerships throughout Scripture. The first partners were Adam and Eve. The Lord did not feel Adam was complete on his own. There was also the partnership of Moses, Aaron, and Hur. When Moses could no longer hold his arms up—as the Lord had instructed him—Aaron and Hur held them up for him and encouraged him (see Exodus 17:8-13). Elijah and Elisha had a well-known partnership. David and Jonathan provide another example of partners. They stuck together through good times and bad (see I Samuel 18:1-4).

Jesus also set several examples of the buddy system concept. He sent His disciples out two by two and ". . . gave them authority over evil spirits" (Mark 6:7). He sent two disciples to find a place to hold the Passover meal just before His death (see Mark 14:13-15). In Luke 10 Jesus appointed 72 other disciples and sent them out in pairs. Paul also often had a partner in his missionary travels.

Just as a kindergartner's buddy will hold him accountable and maybe point out interesting things on a trip, a prayer partner will do the same for you. Your prayer partner will be there to encourage you when you feel like quitting. He or she will confirm things the Lord is showing you and will help you see more as you are praying out in the field.

As you can see, there are numerous examples of the use of partners. Prayer partners are invaluable. I know I wouldn't trade my prayer partner for the world. Please take advantage of the benefits of a prayer partner as you work at possessing the land.

Be faithful to pray with your prayer partner. You may want to start by setting a specific time aside to spend with him or her. You can share what the Lord has been doing in your life and what He has been revealing to you. Then the two (or more) of you can pray concerning these things. The relationship will grow from there. Remember, God's word says that ". . . where two or three come together in my name, there am I with them" (Matthew 18:20).

It is not necessary to limit this partnership to only two. You could also form a trio or maybe even a foursome, but I wouldn't recommend more than that.

Two are better than one, because they have a good return for their work: If one falls down, his friend can help him up. But pity the man who falls and has no one to help him up! Also, if two lie down together, they will keep warm. But how can one keep warm alone? Though one may be overpowered, two can defend themselves. A cord of three strands is not quickly broken. (Ecclesiastes 4:9-12)

You need to have at least one prayer partner. Limit the number of prayer partners to a very small number in order to provide the intimacy needed.

 ## Prayer Activity

Call your prayer partner and set up a time to get together for prayer.

I am meeting with my prayer partner(s) on

_____ at _____am/pm at

_____.

STEP 3:
Join a Local Prayer Group

In the book of Acts we read time and again of the early Christians meeting in someone's home for prayer. The Lord always moved mightily as a result of these times of prayer. A home prayer group is a great place to share your commitment to possessing the land. Others in your group may even feel led to join you in the work. If you know of no prayer groups to join, consider starting one yourself.

There are several types of home prayer groups. Here are a few examples:

Neighborhood Houses of Prayer (NHOP)

Neighborhood Houses of Prayer are impacting neighborhoods across the world. An NHOP is made up of residents within a neighborhood who come together regularly to pray for their neighbors. As neighbors are prayed for and their needs met through prayer they are drawn to Jesus. Thus, the NHOP becomes known as the place to go if someone has a need in his or her life. NHOPs are usually open to all neighbors whether Christian or not and therefore also provide excellent evangelism opportunities.

You might consider starting or joining an NHOP in your neighborhood. They serve as great strongholds for God throughout the land, and when enough of the Lord's strongholds exist, the enemy's strongholds are destroyed. Refer to the resource section of the manual to find where to get more information on starting a Neighborhood House of Prayer.

Cell Groups

Some congregations have what is called a cell-group ministry. Cell groups are designed to provide fellowship, discipleship, encouragement, and accountability in a small-group atmosphere. It's a great place for sharing the work of possessing the land, and the cell group could join you in the area of land you are working as well as work in other pieces of land.

Some churches actually call their cell groups Houses of Prayer. This affords the opportunity to combine the encouragement and other elements offered in a cell group with the opportunity to pray for and reach out to neighborhoods and communities. A church with several NHOPs or cell groups committed to taking possession of the land will have a large impact on the community.

Area-Wide Prayer Groups

On a larger scale, there are other prayer groups that usually consist of representatives from several churches and denominations who come together to pray for the city. It is like a prayer/cell group for the churches of the city. Talk to other people who are interested or involved in prayer ministry and see if any groups like this exist in your area.

Several denominations and churches coming together like this form a mighty stronghold for our Lord. Walls between the denominations are broken down, paving the way for increased unity in the body of Christ. This unity is very important. Do some checking around and see what is going on in your area. The Lord may have you start area-wide prayer groups.

The prayer groups described above can follow the same strategy set forth in this manual. Individuals would work through the first three phases on their own, and the group could then come together and possibly join other groups to carry out the remainder of the phases. This would greatly impact your land because not only would an individual or church possess the land, but the body of Christ would be working in unity to advance the Lord's work of possessing the land.

 ## Journal Entry

The following prayer groups already meet in my area:

_____

_____

_____

The Lord is leading me to join or start the following prayer group(s):

_____

_____

_____

Joining other Christians in the city to take possession of the land sets up "beachheads" throughout the land, which become strategic points from which the Lord works. These groups make it much harder for our enemy, Satan, to have possession of the land because he and his forces get crowded out.

PHASE V
Establish the Borders

STEP 1:
Tear Down the Walls

Perhaps the enemy has built walls around or throughout your property that need to fall down. Just as Joshua led the Israelites to march around Jericho, the Lord may lead you to walk around all or part of your property, tearing down walls that should not be there. Enlist your prayer partner and/or others to join you in this. Yet, just as with anything else only do it if prompted by the Lord, and if prompted follow His direction. And be sure to go through your equipment/checklist before you begin.

Walls built by the enemy could be present either to attempt to keep the Lord out or to keep the forces of darkness in. If the Lord leads you to deal with these walls do so remembering that it is Christ within you doing the work. Satan has no authority over you if you have accepted the Lord as Savior and have gone through the process of consecrating yourself. If you have been faithful to remove anything that is unpleasing to the Lord from your life the enemy is powerless over you.

Be sensitive to the Holy Spirit and step out in faith. He only asks for your obedience. He will do the rest.

Bible Reading

Read Joshua 6 then answer the following questions.

1. Who presented the plan of tearing down the walls of Jericho?

2. Why were the walls around Jericho an issue?

3. What did Joshua tell the priests to take up on the first day? See verse 6. This item would have represented the presence of the Lord.

4. Why were the people to shout the seventh time around? See verse 16.

STEP 2:
Restore the Walls

With the heirs of the land working together and establishing beachheads or prayer groups throughout the land we can now establish the borders. Borders need to be established around the tracts of land in which the Lord is calling individuals to work, but they also need to be set up around larger pieces of land that the body is working in as a team. To establish these borders, the Lord may lead you to do one or more of the things mentioned here or something unique to your situation.

Just as the Lord may lead you to tear down walls of the enemy, He may also tell you to establish borders by building and/or restoring walls around your land. These spiritual walls are built to protect the inhabitants from the enemy and provide common ground in which we can all work in unity. They are not like the walls we build up between ourselves based on our differences; rather, they are built based on the similarities and unity we have among us.

There is a great example of rebuilding a wall in Scripture. Complete the following activity to learn how one man of God went about building a wall. We can learn from this example:

 **Bible Reading**
Read Nehemiah 1-6.

  1. Who was Nehemiah?

2. What was he called by God to do?

3. Who had destroyed the original wall?

4. When opposition came how did Nehemiah and the workers handle it?

5. What did the wall provide for the inhabitants?

More than likely the Lord will not call you to build a physical wall around your land, but He may lead you to build a spiritual wall. This spiritual wall will be built by a physical action you take that will have an impact in the spiritual realm.

The physical action could be walking or driving around the perimeter of your land. As you travel around the property you can proclaim that the Lord Jesus Christ is the true owner. Praise the Lord for His righteousness and protection, for it is this righteousness and protection that forms the wall around your land. Let the Holy Spirit prompt you what to pray. If He leads you to travel the borders of your land without saying a word then do that. Your act of faith and obedience will make an impact in the spiritual realm. The enemy will know you are acting upon the Lord's command.

Prayer Activity

Everyone following this strategy has been called to possess the land where his or her home sits. Even if you are unclear of how far out to go from that land, you know this piece of land is yours. Let's practice tearing down and building walls.

1. Tear down ungodly walls around your home and property.
    a. Spend time in prayer before going out, allowing the Lord to purify you.
    b. Walk around your property and home seven times like Joshua.
       * Be quiet as you go. Listen to God. Pray what He prompts you to.
       * Try walking counterclockwise as a representation of tearing down.

2. Build a wall of righteousness.
    a. Walk around your property three times (clockwise this time)
       * Each time around will represent the Trinity and a cord of three strands.

3. Quote promises from God's word regarding your land.

4. Praise God for the protection of His walls.

5. Do what the Lord leads you to.

Journal Entry

Record anything you discover or anything the Lord
is leading you to do following the previous activity.

_____

_____

_____

_____

_____

_____

_____

_____

_____

_____

_____

Step 3:
Divide the Land

After the Israelites crossed the Jordan to possess the promised land, the Lord had the land divided up. Each tribe took possession of its piece of property and settled on it. Depending on the size of your property it can be divided into several parts and assigned to different groups and individuals. In Joshua 18 the Lord told Joshua to divide the land into parts. He may have already had you do that, too. Dividing the land may be something the Lord is just now showing you to do. If He does lead you to divide the land do not panic. It is not as difficult as it seems. Fighting for possession of the land will be much more manageable if the land is divided into parts.

Whether you are possessing a large tract of land or a smaller one, it can be divided. A city or county can be divided into zip codes, which can be divided into neighborhoods. Neighborhoods can then be broken down street by street and even home by home. If the Lord has led you to begin working on a small tract of land for the time being, don't worry. You are doing what the Holy Spirit has led you to do. Your land may not need to be divided, but you may later find others working plots of land near or adjacent to yours. You can then start working with these people to possess the larger piece of land. In this case the division would have already taken place and each of you would have already been working your assignment. If the Lord at a later date prompts you to possess more land, you may find it necessary to apply the concept of dividing the land. Each of us just needs to be sure we are doing our part.

For those of you who do have large tracts of land to possess, there are many great tools that can be used in dividing the land and assigning troops to each part. There is computer software available that was developed to do just this very thing. The software is called "Kingdom Combine" and is produced by The National Mapping Center for Evangelism. Information on how to get this software is in the Resource section of this book.

Once you have divided the land you will assign troops to each part. Perhaps a church or group of churches would like to cover a zip code. Cell groups or NHOPs may want to cover a neighborhood or even several neighborhoods. Individuals may also want to cover a neighborhood. Individuals can definitely cover a street or block. Everyone can cover at least one home other than his or her own. When the task is divided into smaller portions it is much easier and more manageable for the body as a whole to work together. If you do not feel the Lord leading you to do this do not worry. As you are out meeting others who are called to pray for your city you may find someone else is already doing it. Remember, each of us has a part to play. Do not take on tasks without the Lord's leading; you may be cheating someone else out of being used by the Lord.

It is crucial that you continue to spend time with the Lord, hearing your orders from Him. He sees the "big picture" and knows what He has assigned to whom. You be diligent at the things He calls you to do. Again, obedience is the key. It is not how much you do, but how obedient you are that is important.

PHASE IV & V
Progress Report

Date: _____

Directions: Check all activities that have been completed.

_____ 1.   I have read Numbers 32.

_____ 2.   I have met with my prayer partner at least once.

_____ 3.   I have sought out other prayer group(s) to join.

_____ 4.   I have torn down spiritual walls around my home.

_____ 5.   I have restored any broken walls around my home.

_____ 6.   I have divided the land.

Note: This checklist is a little different. The first three items should be completed, but the other items do not necessarily have to be. You should be working on and praying about the last three.

PHASE VI
Proclaim Ownership

STEP 1:
Proclaim Ownership

As you are out building walls, establishing borders, setting up beachheads, surveying, etc., you are acting upon the Lord's promise that the He ". . . will give you every place where you set your foot . . ." Joshua 1:3. He has given you this land.

It is a good idea to take time to proclaim that, though you have possibly been doing that all along. Following are a couple of examples of how heirs of the Kingdom have proclaimed ownership of the land given to them by the Lord.

Sign a Covenant

Signing a covenant or contract is one way to proclaim ownership. You can write your own covenant or use one that has been written by others. You also may sign the covenant just on your own or invite others to join you.

In the area where I live this covenant has been signed by many of those committed to possessing the land. It represents our commitment to possessing the land and informs the enemy of his eviction.

Our Covenant

We the undersigned do hereby purchase the city of
_____ . We are acting upon
the direction of the Lord God Almighty to buy this land
from the current occupant. The land is now to be cared for,
plowed, and tended as fertile ground for the Lord's harvest.

Jesus Christ has given us authority to purchase this land
with the blood He shed on Calvary. Upon the signing of this
contract all properties and residents will become property of
the Kingdom of God. All trespassers will be removed. The
land will be redeemed to its original purpose of reaching the
lost with the Gospel of Jesus Christ.

Upon signing this document I commit myself to participate in taking possession of this land in unity with all other
members of the body of Christ in   (Insert name of your
land.)

Signed _____

Date _____

A full-page copy of this is provided in the back of this manual.

Please do not sign a covenant like this unless you mean it. God made a covenant with the children of Israel. They were to worship only Him and they would be delivered into the promised land. Yet the Israelites did not live up to their end of the bargain. The Old Testament is full of accounts of their wandering in the wilderness, being taken into captivity, and dying because of their failure to fulfill their covenant with God. A covenant with God is not to be taken lightly. In Deuteronomy 30 Moses speaks to the Israelites of the consequences of their breaking their covenant with God. Please take time to read this passage before entering a covenant with the Lord.

Stake a Claim

In one city simultaneous services were held at the four corners of the city. Stakes were driven into the ground to represent land ownership much like land prospectors did when settlers of the West claimed land in the 1800s. This was a physical act representing the Body of Christ's commitment to owning the land. Representatives from numerous churches and denominations participated.

Christians in other cities and communities are doing similar things to proclaim ownership of their land. These are just a couple of ideas. Use them if the Lord leads you to, but if He leads you to do different things, or nothing at this time, then do that.

 Journal Entry

Record how the Lord may be leading you to proclaim ownership of your land.

_____

_____

_____

_____

_____

_____

_____

_____

_____

_____

PHASE VII
Meet the Inhabitants

STEP 1:
Walk Among the People

You may have already begun doing this. When you are out in your land make a point of greeting your neighbors. Talk to people as you are out prayerwalking. Do not be afraid to let them know that you are praying for your neighborhood as you are out walking.

Jesus walked among the people all the time, and He never hesitated to let them know that He was about his Father's business. Since Jesus always walked in the Father's will He must have been praying as He walked along. As people came to know who Jesus was they were drawn to Him. They wanted to hear what He had to say and came to Him when they needed advice, healing, deliverance, etc.

If people inhabiting our land see us and know we are out doing God's work they will become curious. As you are out meeting people don't be surprised if someone asks you to pray for them. Most people believe in prayer. They may not all agree on who answers prayer, but they believe in prayer itself. When someone asks you to pray for them it is always a good idea to offer to pray for them at that moment. Let people know you are praying to God the Creator and that it is through Jesus that prayers are answered.

In addition, it may be a good idea to carry a small pocket notebook and pen with you. You may not learn things that need to be written down every time, but it is always a good idea to be prepared.

STEP 2:
Discern the Spiritual Condition of the People

The Lord will reveal many things to you as you are out prayerwalking the land. You will learn quite a bit by simply observing the surroundings. It is usually easy to discern the physical needs of the people, and knowing these physical needs will help in discerning the spiritual needs of the people. Observe the economic status of the area. In areas of higher economic status there is quite often a sense of contentment and complacency. These people are in need of the revelation that they need the Lord. Conversely, poverty-stricken areas are obviously in need of provision and the revelation that there is hope in Jesus.

There are other things that will not be so easy to discern. When you are out walking, ask the Lord to reveal the spiritual condition of the inhabitants. You may be led at times to slow your pace down a bit or stop in order to listen to the Lord. Remember to listen with your heart to the Holy Spirit. As mentioned before, ask the Lord to help you see as He sees and hear as He hears.

The things you observe will help you pray more effectively, whether you are out walking or in your prayer closet. The more we know about the subject of our prayers, the better we can pray.

 Prayer Activity

Go for a prayerwalk on the property God has given you. Make a point of speaking to the people you meet along the way, and try to discern their needs.

Journal Entry

Use this space to record names of people you meet, prayer requests, or any other insight you receive while on your prayerwalk.

_____

_____

_____

_____

_____

_____

_____

_____

_____

_____

_____

STEP 3:
Discover the Prayer Needs of the People

Prayers we pray based on observations we have made will make a difference in the lives of the inhabitants. Every prayer you pray in faith will be answered (see Mark 11:24). The inhabitants, however, may not recognize that prayers are being answered or even being prayed. Most people need to see physical evidence of answered prayer. Even though the Lord may be leading you to pray blessings for people, they more than likely do not recognize God as the source of the blessing.

In order to demonstrate the prayer-answering power of God to the inhabitants, it is helpful to give them the opportunity to tell you what they would like you to pray for. There are many variations of how to learn the specific prayer needs of our neighbors. We will only discuss a few methods here. Be creative and let the Lord show you other ways as well.

Door-to-door is the most systematic and comprehensive way to discover prayer requests. Two of the methods discussed here are normally carried out in a door-to-door fashion. Before going out to talk to neighbors personally it is a good idea to pray for your neighbors to be open to your offers of prayer and the love of Jesus. If you can get a list of their names, you can pray for them by name and possibly greet them by name. The software package mentioned in Phase V, Step 3 will generate such lists. Check with mailing list providers to see what is available, or you can check your local library for any information on how you can get such lists. If a list is not available just pray based on addresses. The Lord knows everyone.

Prayer Activity

Using information you may already have, compose a list of at least 10-20 of the people living in the area you are working to possess. List them below and begin praying for them by name.

Survey Method (Door-to-Door)

The survey method is probably the simplest method of gathering prayer requests. Get a notebook or clipboard to carry with you. Knock on each person's door, and when they come to the door introduce yourself as their neighbor. Tell them you have been praying for the neighborhood and those living there and ask if they have any specific things you can pray for. On your clipboard or in your notebook, record their name, address, and request. You may ask them to keep you posted on any developments or other needs they have. Be sure to leave your name and phone number with them.

If you feel the leading of the Holy Spirit to pray for them then and there, take the opportunity. If not, just record the request. Once you have finished gathering requests go back to your prayer partner, NHOP, prayer group, etc. and pray over the requests. Be sure to pray based on the requests given. Even though you may realize their needs go beyond the physical ones they discussed, having their physical needs met will be what draws them to the Lord. This will allow them to see the answers to prayer. Also, be open to meeting those physical needs yourself, if possible. This will illustrate how Jesus loved the people and met their needs, and will open the door to sharing the Gospel with them.

Prayer Card Method (Door-to-Door)

The prayer card method is very similar to the survey method. It requires a little less personal contact with the inhabitants up front but requires a little more planning and preparation. This method could be combined with the survey method in order to ensure that you contact everyone and they all have the opportunity to request prayer.

The basic procedure of the prayer card method is to leave a card with each of the people, letting them know you are praying for them and would like to pray for their specific needs. You can have a phone number on the card they can call with requests or have them mail the cards to you. You could also explain on the card that you will be back on a specific day to get their requests. If you do the latter be sure to return for the requests.

It is important that you seriously pray for each request given. Follow-up is crucial. Check back with neighbors to see how they are doing, if any prayers have been answered, or if there are any new requests to add. A sample of a prayer card is included in the back of the manual, and you are encouraged to reproduce it.

You do not have to obtain prayer requests from all the occupants at once. If you took the opportunity to divide the land into manageable groups in Phase V, you could apply that step here. The number and size of each group will depend on how many people are working with you. Remember, it is more important to be able to commit quality time to praying for the needs than it is to have large numbers of needs to pray for.

Neighborly Chat Method

Perhaps you would like to undertake a more personal method of gathering prayer requests. If so, the Neighborly Chat method will work well. This is especially effective if the land you are taking possession of is a neighborhood.

As you are out in your neighborhood, strike up conversations with your neighbors and ask if they have any needs you can pray for. If you have a little notebook and pen handy, write down the requests as they are given. This shows your neighbor that you are serious about praying for him. As soon as you walk away begin praying for your neighbor. Add his or her name and request to your regular prayer list as soon as possible, and be sure to

check in with him from time to time to see how things are
going regarding the requests.

If the Holy Spirit prompts you to pray with the person
at that moment do so, but ask your neighbor's permission
first. If he is not agreeable then pray silently as you chat.
If you are part of a cell group or Neighborhood House of
Prayer you may be prompted to invite your neighbor. Offer
the invitation. Even if the neighbor does not accept it will
show your interest in him. As with all the other things you
have done throughout the manual, follow the Holy Spirit's
lead.

Prayer Activity

Choose one of the three methods discussed in this
step. Set two dates with your prayer partner, prayer
group, etc. to:

1. Pray for neighbors in general before making
    contact with them.

2. Go out into the land either leaving prayer cards
    or gathering requests via the survey or neigh-
    borly chat method.

You may want to set a follow-up date with your team.

Record your plans for this activity here:

Method chosen

_____survey   _____cards   _____combination

Who is responsible for supplies?

_____

Date of first meeting to pray for neighbors on list:

_____

Date to go out into the land gathering requests:

_____

Date to pray as a team for these requests:

_____

Follow-up date: _____

As you are out gathering prayer requests you will learn of other Christians in the area. As you get the opportunity to meet them, invite them to join you and the others working with you. This will increase the unity among believers.

You will also learn of homes and areas where occultic or otherwise evil activities take place. These are enemy strongholds. You will want to pray that they be changed into the Lord's strongholds through the truth of His Gospel.

Remember to make note of both types of strongholds in your journal and on your maps.

PHASE VI & VII
Progress Report

Date: _____

Directions: Check all activities that have been completed.

_____ 1. Have chosen a way of proclaiming ownership.

_____ 2. Prayerwalked the land, taking time to talk to the inhabitants.

_____ 3. Made observations of surroundings.

_____ 4. Produced a list of some of the inhabitants.

_____ 5. Set up date for gathering prayer requests.

_____ 6. Gathered prayer requests.

_____ 7. Continuing to pray for prayer requests.

Several of the items on this list will be works in progress at this point. Be sure to check off each one upon completion. Items 1-5 should be completed before moving to the next phase.

PHASE VIII
Evict the Enemy

Throughout the phases of this strategy you have been
serving notice of the ultimate eviction of the enemy.
Through your prayers, unity with other believers, acts of
obedience, etc. you have put Satan, our enemy, on notice.
Satan claims that the world ". . . has been given to me . .
." (Luke 4:6). This happened when Adam sinned. Satan
and his forces have been occupying this land, striving to
keep the Gospel of Christ suppressed.

Since you as an heir with Jesus are taking possession
of the land the Lord has given you, Satan can no longer
stay. He is like a squatter who moves into unoccupied
territory assuming it is his for the taking. By claiming
ownership you have rendered all of Satan's claims void.
The Body of Christ is moving into the land. Satan our
enemy and his powers of darkness have two choices: They
can either bow their knee to Jesus or leave.

When a tenant is evicted from a dwelling, an eviction
notice is served. The only way to avoid the eviction is to
meet the terms of payment for the dwelling. The payment
for this particular land you have been working to possess
is bowing of the knee and proclaiming Jesus as Lord.

Serve the Eviction Notice!
It is time to serve the eviction notice. If you have
already begun doing this, great! Keep it up. This phase
will reinforce what you have already been doing. You may
find that you will begin to use the information gathered on
strongholds on your land. The Lord may lead you to pray
in specific places serving eviction notices. Be sure to put
on your armor and take a prayer partner along when you
go out to serve eviction notices on land in which Satan has
established strongholds.

As you are prayerwalking and meeting inhabitants,
inform Satan and his forces that they may no longer oc-

cupy this area. Remind him that the land has been claimed for Jesus and is being occupied by the children of God. Proclaim that the light of Jesus and the power of the Holy Spirit are present. Remind him that he cannot dwell where they are.

Pray blessings upon the land and its occupants. Worship the true owner as you pray or prayerwalk. It is okay to sing as you are walking along. Psalm 47 tells us that God subdued the nations and chose our inheritance for us. We are then encouraged to ". . . sing praises to God, sing praises; sing praises to our King, sing praises" (Psalm 47:6).

Use Scripture as you pray for the land. Claim promises that God has made to His people regarding the promised land. Speak the truth of Jesus and who He is. When we pray Scripture we know we are praying God's will because He wrote the words. Make use of the many prayer guides that are available.

 ## Prayer Activity

Ask the Lord to show you where and how to begin serving the eviction notice. Ask if you are to walk throughout the land serving it or if you are to serve a notice at different sites individually.

1. Take time now to pray regarding this.

2. Record how the Lord is directing you to serve the eviction notice.

Use the following example along with anything else the Lord gives you to begin serving the eviction notice.

Sample Prayer

Because of the authority given to me through the blood of Jesus, I serve notice to Satan and all the spirits of darkness in this place that you may no longer dwell here. The light of Jesus is shining in this place and you cannot remain where the Light is. You must either submit to the gospel of Christ and confess him as King of kings and Lord of lords or leave. You must leave the premises immediately.

Father, thank you for the cleansing power of Jesus. Thank you for returning this land to your purposes. May your kingdom increase here. Amen.

PHASE IX
Secure and Expand the Land

STEP 1:
Secure the Borders

You have moved into the land and begun to take up residence. You have met the other occupants and evicted the enemy. It is now time to secure the borders you have established around the land.

These borders were established when you restored or built the walls and divided the land in Phase V. Securing the borders will keep the enemy you just evicted from returning, and it will be a continuing process. Some ways you will secure the borders are:

- ✔ Linking up with other Christians
- ✔ Praying for the needs of inhabitants
- ✔ Following up on the prayer requests
- ✔ Inviting neighbors to join prayer groups, church, etc.
- ✔ Continuing to pray
- ✔ Continuing to walk the land

As long as you live in the land the Lord has called you to for this time in your life, you will find yourself working to secure the borders. The process you have followed up until now will be repeated several times at different levels. The process continues until all the inhabitants of the land receive Christ as Savior.

Because this is a continuous process, consecrating yourself before beginning the work is very important. You will want to continue to keep your heart clean and your life set apart for service in His kingdom. When you feel like giving up, just meditate on verses like these:

In all my prayers for all of you, I always pray with joy because of your partnership in the gospel from the first day until now, being confident of this, that he who began a good work in you will carry it onto completion until the day of Christ Jesus. (Philippians 1:4-6)

Therefore, since we are surrounded by such a great cloud of witnesses, let us throw off everything that hinders and the sin that so easily entangles, and let us run with perseverance the race marked out for us. (Hebrews 12:1)

This is what the Lord says: 'You say about this place, "It is desolate waste, without men or animals." Yet in the towns of Judah and the streets of Jerusalem that are deserted, inhabited by neither men nor animals, there will be heard once more the sounds of joy and gladness, the voices of bride and bridegroom, and the voices of those who bring thank offerings to the house of the LORD, saying, 'Give thanks to the LORD Almighty, for the Lord is good; His love endures forever.' For I will restore the fortunes of the land as they were before, says the LORD. (Jeremiah 33:10-11)

Bible Reading
Read Jeremiah 33.

1. Where was Jeremiah when the Lord spoke to him in verse 2?

2. As far as Jeremiah was concerned, did it look like there was much hope for the city?

3. Were Jeremiah's views the same as the Lord's? Explain.

4. Who does the Lord say will restore the land?

Jeremiah was in a very hopeless place according to man's eyes. He was in prison for prophesying truth. I am sure he felt he was not making a difference, but the Lord saw the big picture. The Lord saw the plans He had for the city, and He reminded Jeremiah that He would restore the land.

The Lord is the same today as He was then. He only requires that we be obedient just as Jeremiah was. Even though things will not always look promising we must remember the sovereign power of our God. He restores the land, and we have to be willing to be used by Him to do that.

Step 2:
Extend the Borders

We have gone in and taken possession of the land. It has been tilled and plowed through prayer, watered by the love of Jesus, and seeds have been planted along the way. It is time to extend the borders, but we need more workers to do this. All the known Christians should already be working with us, so where do we go to get more workers for the field? This brings us to the step that is really the purpose of everything we have done so far. That purpose is to share the Gospel with the lost.

The field has been plowed through our prayers and some seeds have been planted as we have been out working. It is now time to plant more seeds, water the land, and harvest the crops. Each time a crop is harvested more workers are added to the field. This allows us to extend our borders. Evangelism is the method used for doing that.

We can evangelize in a variety of ways. For example, all of us should already be practicing lifestyle evangelism. We should be living our lives in a way that sets us apart, causing others to be curious as to why we are different. We should also be taking every opportunity to talk about Jesus. In this way we are sowing those seeds and making ourselves available for the harvest at all times.

We can also share the Gospel through the use of tracts. Just as we went around asking for the prayer requests of our neighbors, we can go around giving them a Gospel tract. It is always a good idea to give something along with the tract, like a loaf of bread. The message of the Bread of Life delivered with a loaf of bread can have a great impact on someone.

You can also take advantage of holidays that cause people to think more about God. Invite people over for a viewing of the "Jesus" film or other Christian video. Give out little cards or gifts that have Scripture on them.

Take every opportunity to invite people to join you at church, for prayer meetings, etc. Also, never underestimate the power of sharing a cup of coffee or tea with someone. Opening our homes to others is one of the greatest things we can do to draw others to Christ. They will see how we live our lives as children of God and want what we have in our relationship with Christ.

The key is to love our neighbors so much that they realize they cannot live without Jesus. If we have effectively plowed the field while we have been praying for the inhabitants of the land, a harvest is inevitable. The Lord will bring the increase.

Prayer Activity

Take time now to ask the Lord if there is anything specific He would have you do in your land to evangelize the lost. He may have you just reach out to one person. He may have you plan an event involving many people. Once again, be quiet before the Lord and let Him reveal His plan of evangelism to you for your land.

Journal Entry

Record what the Lord shared with you as you prayed about an evangelism strategy. You may either record it here or in your personal journal.

_____

_____

_____

_____

_____

_____

_____

As you share the Gospel by whatever means the Lord
leads you to, harvesting souls will be the result. These
souls can then be trained to work in His Kingdom. As the
number of Christian occupants increases, you will be able
to purchase more land beyond your original piece.

Don't forget to maintain your original piece of land
periodically, repeating the cycle there. As several people
in numerous areas repeat the cycle, the entire population
will become children of God. Then we can cross over into
the true promised land of heaven, where we will see our
precious Jesus face to face.

As we each join in this strategy, the way of the Lord
will be prepared as the lost are drawn to Him. The Lord's

return will come only after the Gospel has been shared with the whole world, according to Matthew 24:14. So let us take possession of the land spiritually so we may soon move into our true promised land with the King.

I pray blessings, courage and strength for you as you go out to possess the land your Father has given you. The Lord wants to do mighty things through you as you go out to take possession of the land.

Remember, this is a strategy that is to be applied several times over. Now that you have completed the manual, continue applying the principles as you fulfill your commission to reach the lost with the Gospel of Jesus Christ.

RESOURCES AND TOOLS

Ministries Offering Resources and Tools

Below you will find information on how to contact organizations and ministries about the many resources and
concepts mentioned throughout this manual.

Neighborhood Houses of Prayer
P.O. Box 141312
Grand Rapids, MI 49514
Phone: 1-800-217-5200

Offers training materials and resources for starting a
Neighborhood House of Prayer.

Waymakers "Preparing God's Way by Prayer"
Box 203131
Austin, TX 78720-3131
Phone: 512-419-7729 or 419-PRAY
Fax: 512-219-1999
Web: www.waymakers.org

Offers many resources such as the ones below:

Seek God for the City
A 40-day prayer guide for spiritual awakening
designed to focus prayer for the whole city during
the 40 days leading up to Palm Sunday. A revised
version published annually. 32 pages.

Prompts for Prayerwalkers: Seven Ways to Pray from God's Word for Your World
Pocket-sized booklet puts portions of Scripture and prayer ideas right at your fingertips as you pray on the streets. 16 pages.

PrayerWalk Organizer Guide
A 165-page manual of how to organize citywide prayerwalk efforts.

Prayerwalking: Praying On-Site with Insight
by Steve Hawthorne and Graham Kendrick (Creation House.) A practical menu of proven ideas to begin prayerwalking your area. Stories from more than one hundred prayerwalking Christians will encourage you.

Mapping Center for Evangelism
8615 Rosehill Road, Suite 101
Lenexa, KS 66215-2897
Phone: 888-MAP-7997
Fax: 913-438-7303
Web: www.map4Jesus.org

Offers software called "Kingdom Combine," which generates maps of cities broken down by zip codes and neighborhoods while providing residential listings to be used for the purpose of prayer and evangelism.

National Coordinating Efforts

As Christians we are commissioned to reach the world with the Gospel of Jesus Christ. Mission America offers tools, training, and assistance in sharing the Gospel throughout our communities in a coordinated way. To get more information on how to become a part of this coordinated effort, contact Mission America using the information below:

Mission America
5666 Lincoln Drive, Suite 100
Edina, MN 55436
Phone: 800-995-8572
      952-912-0001
Web: www.missionamerica.org or
     www.lighthousemovement.com
Email: nfrizzell@compuserve.com

More Prayer and Evangelism Ministries

Following are ministries and organizations with a focus on reaching every person with the Gospel through prayer and evangelism. Each one employs different methods of reaching our communities, and they have been grouped here according to those methods.

City-Reaching Strategies

Dawn Ministries
7899 Lexington Drive #200B
Colorado Springs, CO 80920
Phone: 719-548-7460
Fax: 710-548-7475
Email: 71102.2745@compuserve.com

Pray U.S.A.! Prayer Ministry
P.O. Box 27526
San Francisco, CA 94127
Phone: 415-337-7293
Fax: 415-587-7293

March For Jesus U.S.A.
P.O. Box 3216
Austin, TX 78764
Phone: 512-416-0066
Fax: 512-445-5393
Email: 04203.262@compuserve.com
Web: www.mfj.org

National Day of Prayer
P.O. Box 15616
Colorado Springs, CO 80935-5616
Phone: 800-444-8828
or 719-531-3379
Fax: 719-548-4520
Email: ndptf@aol.com
Website: www.ndptf.org

Women's Prayer Groups

AGLOW International
P.O. Box 1749
Edmonds, WA 98020-1749
Phone: 425-755-7282
Fax: 425-778-9615
Email: aglow@aglow.org
Web: www.aglow.org

Prayer and Evangelism

Harvest Evangelism
6155 Almaden Expressway, #400
San Jose, CA 95120
Phone: 408-927-9052
Fax: 408-927-9830
Email: harvevan@aol.com
Web: www.harvestevan.org

Every Home For Christ
P.O. Box 35930
Colorado Springs, CO 80935-3593
Phone: 719-260-8888
Fax: 719-260-7505
Email: info@ehc.org
Web: www.ehc.org

Evelyn Christenson Ministries,Inc.
4265 Brigadoon Drive
St. Paul, MN 55126
Phone: 612-566-5390
Fax: 612-566-5390

World Prayer Center
11005 State Hwy 83, Suite #119
Colorado Springs, CO 80921
Phone: 719-262-9922
Fax: 719-262-9920
Email: info@wpccs.org
Web: www.wpccs.org

Men's Prayer Groups

Promise Keepers
P.O. BOX 103001
Denver, CO 80250-7600
Phone: 303-964-7600
Fax: 303-433-1036
Web: www.promisekeepers.org

Prayer for Government Leaders

Intercessors for America
P.O. Box 4477
Leesburg, VA 20177-8155
Phone: 703-777-0003
Fax: 703-777-2324
Email: usapray@aol.com
Web: http://www.ifa-usapray.org/

Lydia Fellowship International
1474 Valcartier Drive
Sunnyvale, CA 94087
Phone: 408-732-2947
Fax: 408-732-2972
Email: tyrna@bahl.com

Prayer for Schools/Teachers

Moms In Touch
P.O. Box 1120
Poway, CA 92074-1120
Phone: 619-486-4065
Fax: 619-486-5132
Email: mitihqtrs@compuserve.com
Web: www.europa.com/ ~ philhow/moms_in_touch.html

Christian Educators Assn. Int'l
P.O. Box 41300
Pasadena, CA 91114-8300
Phone: 626-798-1124
Fax: 626-798-2346
Email: ceaieduca@aol.org
Web: www.ceai.org

See You At The Pole
Web: www.syatp.com

Suggested Reading Materials on Prayer and Evangelism

Prayerwalking: Praying On-Site With Insight
By Steve Hawthorne and Graham Kendrick
(Creation House, 1993)

Taking Our Cities for God
By John Dawson (Creation House, 1989)

Healing America's Wounds
By John Dawson (Regal Books, 1994)

Breaking Strongholds in Your City
Edited by C. Peter Wagner (Regal, 1993)

That None Should Perish
By Ed Silvoso (Regal Books, 1994)

Houses of Prayer: Reaching Cities, One Neighbor at a Time
By Vance Hardisty (Carodyn Publishers, 1993)
Available from Renewal International, P.O. Box 27994, Concord, CA 94527-0994; Phone: 510-685-4846.

Commitment to Conquer: Redeeming Your City by Strategic Intercession
By Bob Beckett and Rebecca Wagner Sytsema (Revell, 1997)

Permission for Reproduction of Tools

Tools have been included in this manual for you to use in taking possession of the land by prayer and evangelism throughout our communities. As a part of this manual, these items are protected under copyright laws. Permission is given below to reproduce the tools on the following pages. Please use these freely for the purpose of prayer and evangelism while adhering to the parameters in the statement of permission to reproduce.

Written permission must be obtained to reproduce any material prior to this page of the manual.

Permission for Reproduction

The author, Cindy Tosto, and the publisher, Wagner Publications hereby give permission to the owner of this copy of *Taking Possession of the Land: A Step-by-Step Guide to Transforming Your Neighborhood Through Strategic Prayer,* to reproduce the included covenant, prayer cards, and prayer guide for prayerwalking for the purpose of prayer and evangelism. These pages may not be used for resale or enhancement of any other product sold without prior authorization from the author/publisher. The author and publisher can be contacted using information on the copyright page.

Instructions for Reproduction

Instructions for Reproduction of Prayer Cards

1. For best results, obtain perforated door hanger card stock from your local office supply retailer. (If this type of card stock is unavailable, regular card stock may be used. You can punch a hold in the top of each card and slip a rubber band through to provide a way to hang the card on doorknobs.)

2. Make at least one copy of the cards separate from this book.

3. Make double-sided copies of the originals onto card stock as described in step #1.

4. Using a paper cutter, cut the cards evenly.

5. Insert name and phone number to contact with prayer requests into box on back of card. (This can be done to each card individually or inserted on your original before copies are made.)

6. Pray for those to receive the card.

7. Sign the card.

8. Hang the cards on doors throughout neighborhoods.

9. Prepare for prayer requests to start coming in.

Instructions for Reproduction of Covenant

1. Make a copy of the covenant.

2. Insert the name of your land on the blank.

3. Use on your own as an individual or sign with a group.

4. The Covenant can be enlarged to provide space for several signatures or to be used for display at prayer meetings, etc.

Our Covenant

We the undersigned do hereby purchase the land of
_____. We are acting upon
the direction of the Lord God Almighty to buy this
land from the current occupant. The land is now to
be cared for, plowed, and tended as fertile ground for
the Lord's harvest.

    Jesus Christ has given us authority to purchase
this land with the blood He shed on Calvary. Upon
the signing of this contract all properties and residents
will become property of the Kingdom of God. All
trespassers will be removed.

    The land will be redeemed to its original purpose
of reaching the lost with the Gospel of Jesus Christ.

    Upon signing this document I commit myself to
participate in taking possession of this land in unity
with all other members of the Body of Christ in

_____

_____   _____
        Signed   Date

We believe God hears and answers prayer. We have been praying in the name of Jesus for His blessing on this neighborhood.

We would like to pray more specifically for the needs of our neighbors. Please let us know of any specific things we can pray for.

Your home is being prayed for by:

We believe God hears and answers prayer. We have been praying in the name of Jesus for His blessing on this neighborhood.

We would like to pray more specifically for the needs of our neighbors. Please let us know of any specific things we can pray for.

Your home is being prayed for by:

We believe God hears and answers prayer. We have been praying in the name of Jesus for His blessing on this neighborhood.

We would like to pray more specifically for the needs of our neighbors. Please let us know of any specific things we can pray for.

Your home is being prayed for by:

We believe God hears and answers prayer. We have been praying in the name of Jesus for His blessing on this neighborhood.

We would like to pray more specifically for the needs of our neighbors. Please let us know of any specific things we can pray for.

Your home is being prayed for by:

We believe God hears and answers prayer. We have been praying in the name of Jesus for His blessing on this neighborhood.

We would like to pray more specifically for the needs of our neighbors. Please let us know of any specific things we can pray for.

Your home is being prayed for by:

We believe God hears and answers prayer. We have been praying in the name of Jesus for His blessing on this neighborhood.

We would like to pray more specifically for the needs of our neighbors. Please let us know of any specific things we can pray for.

Your home is being prayed for by:

WE ARE PRAYING FOR YOU AND YOUR FAMILY!

"Touching every home with Christ through prayer"

WE ARE PRAYING FOR YOU AND YOUR FAMILY!

"Touching every home with Christ through prayer"

WE ARE PRAYING FOR YOU AND YOUR FAMILY!

"Touching every home with Christ through prayer"

WE ARE PRAYING FOR YOU AND YOUR FAMILY!

"Touching every home with Christ through prayer"